DEAR CREATIVE

PROMPTS TO HELP YOU NAVIGATE YOUR WILDERNESS PERIOD

CRYSTAL JUDKINS

TWO PENS AND A GRIND PUBLICATIONS

DEAR CREATIVE,

Copyright © 2025 Crystal Judkins. All rights reserved.

Published by Crystal Judkins / Two Pens and a Grind Publications

ISBN: 978-0-9978304-2-2

No part of this publication may be reproduced, distributed, or transmitted in any form or by any means, including photocopying, recording, or other electronic or mechanical methods, without the prior written permission of the publisher, except in the case of brief quotations embodied in critical reviews and certain other non-commercial uses permitted by copyright law. For permission requests, please contact Crystal Judkins at xperiencejay@gmail.com.

Disclaimer Notice

This journal is designed for informational and inspirational purposes only and should not be used as a substitute for professional mental health or medical advice. The prompts, exercises, and suggestions provided are meant to encourage personal reflection and creativity. If you are experiencing mental health concerns, please consult a licensed therapist, counselor, or medical professional.

By reading this document, the reader agrees that under no circumstances are the author or publisher responsible for any losses, direct or indirect, incurred as a result of the use of the information contained within this document, including but not limited to errors, omissions, or inaccuracies.

Legal Notice

All content, including but not limited to text, prompts, design, and layout, is protected by copyright law. Unauthorized use, reproduction, or distribution of this material is strictly prohibited and may result in legal action.

DEAR CREATIVE,

THIS BOOK BELONGS TO:

_____

_____

_____

TABLE OF CONTENTS

Introduction

The Waiting Room

Emotional Rollercoaster

Late Bloomers Still Bloom

A Full Time Job and
a Full Time Dream

Feeling Lost in Your Gifts

Lessons From Silence and Stillness

Feeling Unseen

Learning From Doubt and Uncertainty

Navigating Grief

Finding Meaning in the Fog

You Are Enough

Embracing Growth and
Transformation

DEAR CREATIVE,

TABLE OF CONTENTS

Moments of Reflection and Self Discovery

Finding Clarity in Uncertainty

Gaining Insight From Challenges

Self-Compassion and Patience

Mindfulness and Presence

Reconnecting with Joy

Seeking Inspiration

Encouragement and Self Care

Cultivating a Support System

Embracing the Journey

Let's Get Creative

DEAR CREATIVE,

DEAR CREATIVE,

INTRODUCTION

FINDING YOUR WAY THROUGH THE WILDERNESS.

DEAR CREATIVE,

As a full time multi-hyphenate, I've spent a great deal of time overthinking and worrying about my next steps. I've heard a ton of nos and even talked myself out of a few yeses. From anxiety to imposter syndrome, there have been so many moments where I felt like ditching my dream and running back to a more traditional career. But, this isn't about me.

This journal is dedicated to the creative stuck in the " in between," a place I like to call the wilderness.

What is the wilderness period? This is a pivotal moment in your life when you feel completely lost and everything around you goes radio silent. There are no signs, there is no compass. The only thing you have, is you. This can be a very lonely time. Even if you have family and friends who support your creativity, there are times when they simply don't understand.

Prayer and meditation are helpful, as the wilderness period is a necessary part of growth and self discovery. This journal isn't meant to replace either. These prompts are meant as a reflective resource to help you navigate through this time and process exactly what you're feeling.

More than anything, I hope this journal makes things clearer for you. You are not alone. You are worthy and you will absolutely make it through to the other side.

— CRYSTAL

DEAR CREATIVE,

WHAT IS THE WAITING ROOM?

DEAR CREATIVE,

I've come up with all sorts of metaphorical terms to describe what the wilderness period feels like to me, and the waiting room is no different.

The Waiting Room, is an interesting time during the wilderness period, when you literally feel like you're waiting around for something. The problem is, you don't know what it is you're waiting for or what time it's coming.

There is no receptionist at the front desk. No other patrons around. There's only this empty room with a ticking clock and a few chairs. So you sit and wait, occasionally looking over to the door, wondering when they'll finally call your name. Wondering when it's gonna be your turn.

This is a time used for self reflection and introspection, but we often interrupt it with our worrying and overthinking about the future. The Waiting Room isn't meant to scare you, it's an opportunity to escape 'fight or flight' mode and give way to divine timing.

Use this time to focus on your health and wellness, a time to prioritize joy and a time to just be... Do you know who you are outside of your gifts and talents? If not, this is the perfect time to figure it out.

— CRYSTAL

DEAR CREATIVE,

CHAPTER AFFIRMATIONS

I am patient and trust the timing of my life.

Even in stillness, I am moving closer to my purpose.

This waiting period is a space for growth and preparation.

DEAR CREATIVE,

Writing Prompts

DEAR CREATIVE,

DATE:

FINDING PURPOSE IN THE PAUSE

Think about the ways this waiting period might be serving you. What lessons can I learn in this time of stillness? How is this waiting period preparing me for what's next?

THE POWER OF PATIENCE

Reflect on your relationship with patience. How does waiting make you feel? What are some ways you've grown through patience in the past? How can you reframe your waiting period as an act of trust?

REFLECTION

Reflect on the small, subtle lessons this period has brought. Even in the quiet, something is being shaped within you.

PROMPT

DATE:

Take a moment to reflect on the following:

How do you feel about the idea of waiting right now?

What thoughts come up when you think about being in a space where nothing is moving, or it feels like nothing is happening?

What's one thing you've learned while being in the waiting room?

What's something you've been trying to rush through that might actually need more time?

Is there something you've been pushing forward too quickly? How can you honor the time it takes?

What would it look like to be kind to yourself while waiting?

What is one thing you can do today to show yourself compassion while in this period?

CREATIVE PROGRESS TRACKER

DATE:

This tracker is meant to help you track the small steps you take, even if creativity feels absent. It's not about the outcome, but the willingness to show up for yourself each day. If you can't create today, that's okay. Just take note of how you're feeling and what's showing up for you.

Instructions:

- Instead of focusing on finished projects, use this space to reflect on your emotional state and any subtle moments of creative inspiration, even if they're fleeting.

- You don't have to create something every day. This is about honoring your process, not rushing or pushing yourself.

What I Felt This Week	Creative Moments (Even Small Ones)	Challenges/ Barriers	What I've Learned About Myself	Gentle Next Step

Reflection Prompts:

How do I feel today about my creative process?

What is one small thing I can do for myself today, without expectation of producing anything?

What would it feel like to release the pressure of needing to create right now?

MOOD TRACKER

DATE:

This tracker helps you reflect on how you're feeling each day. Remember, it's okay if some days feel off or if inspiration isn't flowing. Your mood is part of your process and it's important to honor it.

Instructions:

Choose a color for each mood.
For each day, color in the corresponding mood based on how you felt.
At the end of the week, reflect on your emotional landscape. Notice patterns, but don't pressure yourself to always be "productive." Sometimes rest is the most important part of the journey.

Mood Key	Mood	Notes
● Inspired ● Calm ● Low ● Uncertain ● Sad		

Mood Key Colors:

● Inspired -
● Calm -
● Low -
● Uncertain -
● Sad -

DEAR CREATIVE,

Emotional Rollercoaster

DEAR CREATIVE,

There are so many emotions associated with the wilderness period. Uncertainty, confusion, sadness, dread, and if I'm being honest, there's also a great deal of hopelessness.

Your creative journey will always have its highs and lows, but the wilderness period can throw you some of the most intense and challenging lows you've ever experienced.

It's so important for you to not only tap into those emotions, but for you to call them by name. That's what makes it real. We spend a lot of time shielding ourselves from these emotions by pretending they don't exist, but that is counterproductive.

In this first set of prompts, you'll have the opportunity to discuss the emotions you've been feeling during this explorative period.

Don't be afraid to tap in!!

— CRYSTAL

DEAR CREATIVE,

CHAPTER AFFIRMATIONS

I honor my emotions as valid and necessary for my journey.

I am capable of riding the waves and finding calm within the chaos.

My feelings are a testament to my resilience and humanity.

DEAR CREATIVE,

Writing Prompts

DATE:

DEAR CREATIVE,

PRESENT EMOTIONS

What emotions are most prevalent during this wilderness period? Write about them in detail.

IDENTIFYING PATTERNS

How does this wilderness period compare to previous ones you've experienced? What patterns do you notice? If this is your first, discuss the highs and lows of this period.

REFLECTION

What triggers or events led to this wilderness period? Can you identify any underlying causes?

PROMPT

DATE:

What does your wilderness period look like? Describe in detail. Feel free to draw, color, or cut and paste photos from a magazine.

CREATIVE PROGRESS TRACKER

DATE:

This tracker is meant to help you track the small steps you take, even if creativity feels absent. It's not about the outcome, but the willingness to show up for yourself each day. If you can't create today, that's okay. Just take note of how you're feeling and what's showing up for you.

Instructions:

- Instead of focusing on finished projects, use this space to reflect on your emotional state and any subtle moments of creative inspiration, even if they're fleeting.

- You don't have to create something every day. This is about honoring your process, not rushing or pushing yourself.

What I Felt This Week	Creative Moments (Even Small Ones)	Challenges/ Barriers	What I've Learned About Myself	Gentle Next Step

Reflection Prompts:

How do I feel today about my creative process?

What is one small thing I can do for myself today, without expectation of producing anything?

What would it feel like to release the pressure of needing to create right now?

MOOD TRACKER

DATE:

This tracker helps you reflect on how you're feeling each day. Remember, it's okay if some days feel off or if inspiration isn't flowing. Your mood is part of your process and it's important to honor it.

Instructions:

Choose a color for each mood.
For each day, color in the corresponding mood based on how you felt.
At the end of the week, reflect on your emotional landscape. Notice patterns, but don't pressure yourself to always be "productive." Sometimes rest is the most important part of the journey.

Mood Key	Mood	Notes
● Inspired ● Calm ● Low ● Uncertain ● Sad		

Mood Key Colors:

● *Inspired -*
● *Calm -*
● *Low -*
● *Uncertain -*
● *Sad -*

DEAR CREATIVE,

Late Bloomers Still Bloom

DEAR CREATIVE,

If I'm being honest, I kinda hate the term "late bloomer." There's this inaccurate assumption that if you don't hit certain "milestones" by a certain age, then something must be wrong.

It is never too late to tap into your purpose. Your gifts will always make room for you, so please don't be discouraged. Divine timing doesn't miss.

Now, that doesn't mean that you just sit around waiting for an opportunity to fall out of the sky, but know that whether you're 25 or 60, when it's your time, it's your time!

You're exactly where you're meant to be in this very moment, and that may not be very encouraging, but if you've made it this far, know that it's far from over!

You're not late, you're simply making a grand entrance and baby, it's the perfect time!

— CRYSTAL

DEAR CREATIVE,

CHAPTER AFFIRMATIONS

My journey unfolds at the perfect time for me.

I celebrate the beauty of blooming, no matter when it happens.

My path is unique, and I am exactly where I need to be.

DEAR CREATIVE,

Writing Prompts

DEAR CREATIVE,

DATE:

LEARNING FROM OTHERS

Reflect on a person who achieved success later in life. What can you learn from their journey?

BENEFITS OF DOING THINGS LATER

What are three benefits you have now that you didn't have when you were younger, and how can they help you in your creative pursuits?

REFLECTION

Write a manifesto for your future self, detailing what you want to achieve regardless of age.

DEAR CREATIVE,

DATE:

IDEAL CREATIVE LIFE

Write about your ideal creative life five years from now. What are you doing, and how do you feel?

EXPLORING THE PROS AND CONS

List the pros and cons of two different paths you are considering. What stands out to you?

REFLECTION

Describe a moment when you felt most in alignment with your purpose. What were you doing, and how can you find that feeling again?

CREATIVE PROGRESS TRACKER

DATE:

This tracker is meant to help you track the small steps you take, even if creativity feels absent. It's not about the outcome, but the willingness to show up for yourself each day. If you can't create today, that's okay. Just take note of how you're feeling and what's showing up for you.

Instructions:

- Instead of focusing on finished projects, use this space to reflect on your emotional state and any subtle moments of creative inspiration, even if they're fleeting.

- You don't have to create something every day. This is about honoring your process, not rushing or pushing yourself.

What I Felt This Week	Creative Moments (Even Small Ones)	Challenges/ Barriers	What I've Learned About Myself	Gentle Next Step

Reflection Prompts:

How do I feel today about my creative process?

What is one small thing I can do for myself today, without expectation of producing anything?

What would it feel like to release the pressure of needing to create right now?

MOOD TRACKER

DATE :

This tracker helps you reflect on how you're feeling each day. Remember, it's okay if some days feel off or if inspiration isn't flowing. Your mood is part of your process and it's important to honor it.

Instructions:

Choose a color for each mood.
For each day, color in the corresponding mood based on how you felt.
At the end of the week, reflect on your emotional landscape. Notice patterns, but don't pressure yourself to always be "productive." Sometimes rest is the most important part of the journey.

Mood Key	Mood	Notes
● Inspired ● Calm ● Low ● Uncertain ● Sad		

Mood Key Colors:

● *Inspired -*
● *Calm -*
● *Low -*
● *Uncertain -*
● *Sad -*

DEAR CREATIVE,

A Full-Time Job and a Full-Time Dream

DEAR CREATIVE,

Working a 9 to 5, while also being a creative, just ain't for the weak. I know firsthand the struggles creatives face trying to make time for their dreams, while also doing the whole career balancing act.

I reached a point where I could no longer dedicate my life to a career that I had outgrown. I made the difficult decision to take a leap and pursue my dreams full time. And while I don't regret it, I absolutely understand why that's not an option for everyone. Hell, it was barely an option for me.

You may be feeling creator's guilt, something that hits many of us when we feel like we're neglecting our gifts, but don't let it discourage you. You are doing the best you can with what you have, and even if you're not, it's ok. Now is the time to implement a few changes to incorporate your creativity.

— CRYSTAL

DEAR CREATIVE,

CHAPTER AFFIRMATIONS

I am building the life I envision, step by step.

My efforts to balance my responsibilities and passions are worth it.

I have the strength and perseverance to honor both my work and my dreams.

DEAR CREATIVE,

Writing Prompts

DEAR CREATIVE,

DATE:

BALANCING PASSION AND RESPONSIBILITY

Write about the times when your dream and your job feel in conflict. How do you juggle both? How does each one shape who you are and where you're going?

THE ROLE OF SACRIFICE

What sacrifices have you made (or are willing to make) to pursue both your job and your dream? How do you feel about these sacrifices, and do they feel worth it in the grand scheme of things?

REFLECTION

What does a typical day look like for you balancing your full-time job and your full-time dream? Write about the moments when you've managed to carve out time for your passion, no matter how small. How does it feel to dedicate time to your dream in the midst of your work commitments?

WRITING PROMPT

DATE:

Balancing a full-time job and a full-time dream is no easy feat. It's a constant juggle between responsibilities, time, and energy. But what if your dreams didn't have to wait for your job to be over? Reflect on the following:

What does your dream look like in its most vibrant and expansive form?

_____

_____

_____

What parts of your job are feeding your creative dreams, even if they don't seem directly related?

_____

_____

_____

When you think about your dream, what small action can you take today that aligns with where you want to go?

_____

_____

_____

How can you create space within your busy schedule to nurture your creativity without feeling overwhelmed?

_____

_____

_____

Allow yourself to reflect on the tension between practicality and passion. Your dream is already a part of you—how can you honor both your reality and your aspirations today?

_____

_____

_____

CREATIVE PROGRESS TRACKER

DATE:

This tracker is meant to help you track the small steps you take, even if creativity feels absent. It's not about the outcome, but the willingness to show up for yourself each day. If you can't create today, that's okay. Just take note of how you're feeling and what's showing up for you.

Instructions:

- Instead of focusing on finished projects, use this space to reflect on your emotional state and any subtle moments of creative inspiration, even if they're fleeting.

- You don't have to create something every day. This is about honoring your process, not rushing or pushing yourself.

What I Felt This Week	Creative Moments (Even Small Ones)	Challenges/ Barriers	What I've Learned About Myself	Gentle Next Step

Reflection Prompts:

How do I feel today about my creative process?

What is one small thing I can do for myself today, without expectation of producing anything?

What would it feel like to release the pressure of needing to create right now?

MOOD TRACKER

DATE :

This tracker helps you reflect on how you're feeling each day. Remember, it's okay if some days feel off or if inspiration isn't flowing. Your mood is part of your process and it's important to honor it.

Instructions:

Choose a color for each mood.
For each day, color in the corresponding mood based on how you felt.
At the end of the week, reflect on your emotional landscape. Notice patterns, but don't pressure yourself to always be "productive." Sometimes rest is the most important part of the journey.

Mood Key	Mood	Notes
● Inspired ● Calm ● Low ● Uncertain ● Sad		

Mood Key Colors:

● *Inspired -*
● *Calm -*
● *Low -*
● *Uncertain -*
● *Sad -*

DEAR CREATIVE,

Feeling Lost in Your Own Gifts

DEAR CREATIVE,

When discussing our gifts and talents, we often neglect to mention those times where our gifts seem almost bigger than us. Those moments when we feel trapped inside the need to perform or create, without having a clear understanding of the purpose it serves. Or the purpose we're supposed to serve.

Even advice from others can seem to just pile onto the feelings of inadequacy and confusion surrounding what weren't meant to do with our gifts and it can be frustrating.

What do you do with a gift that had no instructions on how to use it? Figure it out, right? Easier said than done.

This can be an overwhelming and disorienting experience, especially for those who solely rely on their talents as a source of identity and fulfillment. No shade. I've been there.

During the wilderness period, you may find yourself experiencing moments that cause you to question your purpose or direction in life, and you'll likely experience them more frequently, but that's exactly what this time if for. It's the perfect time to figure it all out.

Who are you outside of your gifts?

DEAR CREATIVE,

CHAPTER AFFIRMATIONS

My creativity is not lost; it is evolving in ways I have yet to understand.

I am allowed to take a pause and rediscover the joy in my gifts.

My talents are unique and valuable, even when I feel unsure.

DEAR CREATIVE,

Writing Prompts

DEAR CREATIVE,

DATE:

CREATIVE INVENTORY

Take inventory of your creative skills and talents. Which ones bring you the most joy, and which ones feel most aligned with who you are?

EXPLORING NEW ACTIVITIES

Write about a creative activity you haven't tried yet but have always been curious about. How can you explore this new avenue?

REFLECTION

Create a vision board or mind map of your creative journey. Where have you been, and where do you want to go next?

PROMPT

DATE:

Who are you outside of your creative gifts? Does such person even exist?
Create a bio without mentioning any of your talents and gifts.

CREATIVE PROGRESS TRACKER

DATE:

This tracker is meant to help you track the small steps you take, even if creativity feels absent. It's not about the outcome, but the willingness to show up for yourself each day. If you can't create today, that's okay. Just take note of how you're feeling and what's showing up for you.

Instructions:

- Instead of focusing on finished projects, use this space to reflect on your emotional state and any subtle moments of creative inspiration, even if they're fleeting.

- You don't have to create something every day. This is about honoring your process, not rushing or pushing yourself.

What I Felt This Week	Creative Moments (Even Small Ones)	Challenges/ Barriers	What I've Learned About Myself	Gentle Next Step

Reflection Prompts:

How do I feel today about my creative process?

What is one small thing I can do for myself today, without expectation of producing anything?

What would it feel like to release the pressure of needing to create right now?

MOOD TRACKER

DATE:

This tracker helps you reflect on how you're feeling each day. Remember, it's okay if some days feel off or if inspiration isn't flowing. Your mood is part of your process and it's important to honor it.

Instructions:

Choose a color for each mood.
For each day, color in the corresponding mood based on how you felt.
At the end of the week, reflect on your emotional landscape. Notice patterns, but don't pressure yourself to always be "productive." Sometimes rest is the most important part of the journey.

Mood Key	Mood	Notes
● Inspired ● Calm ● Low ● Uncertain ● Sad		

Mood Key Colors:

● *Inspired -*
● *Calm -*
● *Low -*
● *Uncertain -*
● *Sad -*

DEAR CREATIVE,

Lessons from Silence and Stillness

DEAR CREATIVE,

When things go radio silent, it's normal to feel like God, the universe, or whatever religious/spiritual entity or deity you subscribe to (if any), has forgotten about you. Your prayers seem blocked; it literally feels like someone cut the cord to the mainline and all access to the divine has been lost.

You may even feel abandoned by family and friends or at the very least, detached from them. It's almost as if you don't belong anywhere, anymore. Goals may feel out of reach and everything around you feels completely foreign.

...and this of course, subsequently throws you into a series of overthinking, worrying, and doubting yourself until life becomes this overwhelming cycle of confusion that you can't escape. Been there.

Although it may absolutely feel like it, it's important to note that stillness and silence isn't a punishment. Sometimes we're just so caught up in the bustle of everyday, that we forget to take a moment and unplug.

The beautiful thing about silence is that it's an opportunity to shut up and listen. Your prayers aren't being ignored, maybe the answer finds you in a soft whisper, but you won't hear it over all the noise.

— CRYSTAL

DEAR CREATIVE,

CHAPTER AFFIRMATIONS

In stillness, I find clarity and direction.

The quiet moments are where I reconnect with my true self.

I am grateful for the lessons found in silence.

DEAR CREATIVE,

Writing Prompts

DEAR CREATIVE,

DATE:

RECENT EXPERIENCE	**MOMENTS OF STILLNESS**
When you sit in silence, what thoughts or insights come to you? Describe a recent experience.	*How does stillness affect your creativity and thought process? Write about a moment when you found clarity in stillness.*

REFLECTION

What have you discovered about yourself during quiet moments? Reflect on any new understandings or realizations.

PROMPT

DATE:

What does your creativity look like during moments of silence and stillness. Draw, color, paint or create a collage below.

CREATIVE PROGRESS TRACKER

DATE:

This tracker is meant to help you track the small steps you take, even if creativity feels absent. It's not about the outcome, but the willingness to show up for yourself each day. If you can't create today, that's okay. Just take note of how you're feeling and what's showing up for you.

Instructions:

- *Instead of focusing on finished projects, use this space to reflect on your emotional state and any subtle moments of creative inspiration, even if they're fleeting.*
- *You don't have to create something every day. This is about honoring your process, not rushing or pushing yourself.*

What I Felt This Week	Creative Moments (Even Small Ones)	Challenges/ Barriers	What I've Learned About Myself	Gentle Next Step

Reflection Prompts:

How do I feel today about my creative process?

What is one small thing I can do for myself today, without expectation of producing anything?

What would it feel like to release the pressure of needing to create right now?

MOOD TRACKER

DATE :

This tracker helps you reflect on how you're feeling each day. Remember, it's okay if some days feel off or if inspiration isn't flowing. Your mood is part of your process and it's important to honor it.

Instructions:

Choose a color for each mood.
For each day, color in the corresponding mood based on how you felt.
At the end of the week, reflect on your emotional landscape. Notice patterns, but don't pressure yourself to always be "productive." Sometimes rest is the most important part of the journey.

Mood Key	Mood	Notes
● Inspired ● Calm ● Low ● Uncertain ● Sad		

Mood Key Colors:

● *Inspired -*
● *Calm -*
● *Low -*
● *Uncertain -*
● *Sad -*

DEAR CREATIVE,

Feeling Unseen

DEAR CREATIVE,

As a creative, there have been many times I've felt unseen. You'd think that being the creative one makes you stand out, but in a world where everything feels so oversaturated and microwavable, it's easy to feel overlooked. Your wilderness period is no different—in fact, it may feel like you're utterly invisible, even to the people who you thought really "saw" you. And as much as we like to pretend that being seen doesn't matter, it's a deeply human desire to have our gifts and talents validated. When that doesn't happen, it can feel like everything you're doing is in vain. It's not.

So what if your latest post only got two likes? Keep posting—somebody saw it. So what if your book only made ten sales? Keep writing—somebody read it. You might not want to hear this, but often, being hidden is for our own protection. Don't be upset about being unseen; instead, be prepared. Use this time of invisibility to keep writing, brainstorming, creating, and focusing on what makes you uniquely "you."

I can't remember who told me this, but think about the bread aisle at the grocery store. There are tons of different bread brands, and every single one of them is still in business. They're not worried about the competition or about being seen—because everybody likes bread. Similarly, with creatives. Your gifts will always make room for you and though this might not be your time in the spotlight, please don't fade to black.

— CRYSTAL

DEAR CREATIVE,

CHAPTER AFFIRMATIONS

My worth is not determined by recognition from others.

Even when I feel unseen, I know I am valuable and deserving of love.

My light shines brightly, whether or not it is acknowledged.

DEAR CREATIVE,

Writing Prompts

DEAR CREATIVE,

DATE:

PAST

Describe a time when you felt truly seen and heard. What were the circumstances, and who was involved?

FUTURE

List three ways you can advocate for your own visibility and voice in your creative community.

REFLECTION

Are there any moments in your creative journey where you feel unseen and/or unheard? What is that like? List a few adjectives to describe the feeling. What usually triggers those feelings?

PROMPT

DATE:

Write a letter to yourself from the perspective of someone who deeply admires your work. What would they say to encourage you?

CREATIVE PROGRESS TRACKER

DATE:

This tracker is meant to help you track the small steps you take, even if creativity feels absent. It's not about the outcome, but the willingness to show up for yourself each day. If you can't create today, that's okay. Just take note of how you're feeling and what's showing up for you.

Instructions:

- Instead of focusing on finished projects, use this space to reflect on your emotional state and any subtle moments of creative inspiration, even if they're fleeting.

- You don't have to create something every day. This is about honoring your process, not rushing or pushing yourself.

What I Felt This Week	Creative Moments (Even Small Ones)	Challenges/ Barriers	What I've Learned About Myself	Gentle Next Step

Reflection Prompts:

How do I feel today about my creative process?

What is one small thing I can do for myself today, without expectation of producing anything?

What would it feel like to release the pressure of needing to create right now?

MOOD TRACKER

DATE :

This tracker helps you reflect on how you're feeling each day. Remember, it's okay if some days feel off or if inspiration isn't flowing. Your mood is part of your process and it's important to honor it.

Instructions:

Choose a color for each mood.
For each day, color in the corresponding mood based on how you felt.
At the end of the week, reflect on your emotional landscape. Notice patterns, but don't pressure yourself to always be "productive." Sometimes rest is the most important part of the journey.

Mood Key	Mood	Notes
● Inspired ● Calm ● Low ● Uncertain ● Sad		

Mood Key Colors:

● *Inspired -*
● *Calm -*
● *Low -*
● *Uncertain -*
● *Sad -*

DEAR CREATIVE,

Learning from Doubt and Uncertainty

DEAR CREATIVE,

There are plenty of moments in every creative journey when you have no clue what to do next—or even how to get started. Sometimes, all you have is your talent or a good idea but no real leads, and then, as if on cue, imposter syndrome shows up uninvited, trying to convince you that you're a fraud who shouldn't even be creating anything. I know the feeling all too well. Even creating this journal was a whole process for me because I'd never done anything like it before. I almost talked myself out of it, thinking, "There are so many journals out there—why would mine matter?" But the truth is, I was just letting self-doubt run the show, sabotaging myself, and dragging out a process that could've been finished much sooner.

Now, I'm a firm believer in divine timing, so I know everything happens when it's meant to. But let's be honest: sometimes, we play the biggest role in our own setbacks by letting imposter syndrome's negative, hating ass talk us out of our destiny. Stop that.

— CRYSTAL

DEAR CREATIVE,

CHAPTER AFFIRMATIONS

Uncertainty is an opportunity for growth and discovery.

I trust myself to navigate through doubt with courage and grace.

My strength lies in my ability to adapt and persevere.

DEAR CREATIVE,

Writing Prompts

DEAR CREATIVE,

DATE:

COPING MECHANISMS

How do you typically respond to feelings of doubt and uncertainty? Write about your coping mechanisms.

RESILIENCE

What has doubt taught you about your strengths and resilience? Reflect on a specific instance where you grew from doubt.

REFLECTION

How can you use this period of uncertainty to explore new creative ideas or directions? List a few possibilities.

PROMPT

DATE :

Turn your uncertainty and doubt into a visual representation of growth and transformation. This activity will help you channel the emotions tied to doubt and uncertainty into your creativity, reframing them as powerful drivers for change.

Materials Needed:

Paper or sketchbook
Markers, colored pencils, or paint
A quiet space to reflect
(Optional) music that helps you feel calm or introspective

Reflect: Take a moment to think about a time when you were overwhelmed with doubt or uncertainty, either in your creative work or personal life. How did it feel to be in that space? What was the nature of the doubt you felt? Write down a few words that come to mind when you think of those moments (e.g., lost, anxious, afraid, stagnant, unsure, confused).

Create a Visual Representation: Using the materials listed, create a visual piece that represents that doubt or uncertainty. It can be abstract, using shapes and colors that reflect how doubt makes you feel, or you can illustrate specific moments or symbols related to your experience.

Focus on expressing the emotions you felt during that time.

Use colors that feel connected to uncertainty (e.g., grays, blues, or muted tones), or if you feel like adding a sense of transformation, introduce bright colors where you can see the shift.

If you're working with shapes, consider chaotic, fragmented, or jagged lines that convey instability, or more fluid, gentle curves for feelings of unknown potential.

Reframe Your Doubt: Once you've expressed the doubt visually, reflect on how the uncertainty may have contributed to your growth. Use symbols or imagery within your artwork to represent the transformation or lessons you gained. For example:

Add small images like a sprouting seed to symbolize new beginnings, or a light shining through a dark cloud to show clarity emerging.

Alternatively, incorporate words or phrases that helped you reframe your doubt (e.g., "growth through discomfort," "clarity in time," "trust the process").

Reflect & Journal: Take 10 minutes to journal about the process. How does it feel to transform doubt into something creative? What insights about doubt and uncertainty have you gained from this exercise? Write about how you've changed since that period of uncertainty and what you've learned.

Affirmation: After the activity, write down a personal affirmation for yourself that reinforces your ability to work through uncertainty creatively. Example: "I trust my process, even when I cannot see the outcome."

Reflection Questions:

How does visualizing your doubt help you reframe it?
What did you learn about yourself through this process?
How can you continue to use creativity as a tool to navigate future doubts?

DEAR CREATIVE,

DEAR CREATIVE,

CREATIVE PROGRESS TRACKER

DATE:

This tracker is meant to help you track the small steps you take, even if creativity feels absent. It's not about the outcome, but the willingness to show up for yourself each day. If you can't create today, that's okay. Just take note of how you're feeling and what's showing up for you.

Instructions:

- *Instead of focusing on finished projects, use this space to reflect on your emotional state and any subtle moments of creative inspiration, even if they're fleeting.*

- *You don't have to create something every day. This is about honoring your process, not rushing or pushing yourself.*

What I Felt This Week	Creative Moments (Even Small Ones)	Challenges/ Barriers	What I've Learned About Myself	Gentle Next Step

Reflection Prompts:

How do I feel today about my creative process?

What is one small thing I can do for myself today, without expectation of producing anything?

What would it feel like to release the pressure of needing to create right now?

MOOD TRACKER

DATE :

This tracker helps you reflect on how you're feeling each day. Remember, it's okay if some days feel off or if inspiration isn't flowing. Your mood is part of your process and it's important to honor it.

Instructions:

Choose a color for each mood.
For each day, color in the corresponding mood based on how you felt.
At the end of the week, reflect on your emotional landscape. Notice patterns, but don't pressure yourself to always be "productive." Sometimes rest is the most important part of the journey.

Mood Key	Mood	Notes
● Inspired ● Calm ● Low ● Uncertain ● Sad		

Mood Key Colors:

● *Inspired -*
● *Calm -*
● *Low -*
● *Uncertain -*
● *Sad -*

DEAR CREATIVE,

Navigating Grief

DEAR CREATIVE,

There's so much grief involved in the wilderness period. It's not just the external losses—it's the internal ones, too. To become a whole new person, parts of you must metaphorically die. Everything you once knew, the way you saw the world, even the way you approached your art or your relationships—it all shifts. Life as you knew it no longer exists, or it exists in a completely new way that you're left to navigate.

And let's not forget that life continues to happen even as you're in this transformative phase. Friendships end. Partnerships dissolve. People we love leave us, sometimes through circumstance, and other times through death. Processing grief in the middle of this already tumultuous period can feel unbearable, like you're carrying an impossible weight. But as overwhelming as it may seem, there are ways to navigate this grief. Small things can help—creating rituals to honor what you've lost, journaling to process your feelings, finding solace in a support system, or simply allowing yourself to feel without judgment. Grief is never easy, but it can be a profound teacher if we let it. It forces us to slow down, reflect, and ultimately make space for what's to come.

You don't have to have it all figured out. Just take it one moment at a time. Grieve, but don't give up. There's a future version of you waiting on the other side of this wilderness, stronger and more open than you ever thought possible.

— CRYSTAL

DEAR CREATIVE,

CHAPTER AFFIRMATIONS

I allow myself to feel and process grief in my own way and time.

Even in loss, I am capable of finding moments of peace and hope.

I honor what was, while embracing what can be.

DEAR CREATIVE,

Writing Prompts

DEAR CREATIVE,

DATE:

HONOR THE SILENCE

What has grief taught you about stillness, silence, or slowing down? How can these moments be a source of reflection or renewal?

FINDING MEANING IN LOSS

What lessons, if any, have emerged from your grief? How have these lessons changed you or your perspective?

REFLECTION

Is there a part of your creative journey that you've had to let go of? Write about what it meant to you and how you're finding ways to move forward.

PROMPT

DATE:

If your grief were a color, a texture, or a shape, what would it look like?
Draw it below. How does this imagery help you understand it better?

CREATIVE PROGRESS TRACKER

DATE:

This tracker is meant to help you track the small steps you take, even if creativity feels absent. It's not about the outcome, but the willingness to show up for yourself each day. If you can't create today, that's okay. Just take note of how you're feeling and what's showing up for you.

Instructions:

- Instead of focusing on finished projects, use this space to reflect on your emotional state and any subtle moments of creative inspiration, even if they're fleeting.
- You don't have to create something every day. This is about honoring your process, not rushing or pushing yourself.

What I Felt This Week	Creative Moments (Even Small Ones)	Challenges/ Barriers	What I've Learned About Myself	Gentle Next Step

Reflection Prompts:

How do I feel today about my creative process?

What is one small thing I can do for myself today, without expectation of producing anything?

What would it feel like to release the pressure of needing to create right now?

MOOD TRACKER

DATE:

This tracker helps you reflect on how you're feeling each day. Remember, it's okay if some days feel off or if inspiration isn't flowing. Your mood is part of your process and it's important to honor it.

Instructions:

Choose a color for each mood.
For each day, color in the corresponding mood based on how you felt.
At the end of the week, reflect on your emotional landscape. Notice patterns, but don't pressure yourself to always be "productive." Sometimes rest is the most important part of the journey.

Mood Key	Mood	Notes
● Inspired ● Calm ● Low ● Uncertain ● Sad		

Mood Key Colors:

● *Inspired -*
● *Calm -*
● *Low -*
● *Uncertain -*
● *Sad -*

DEAR CREATIVE,

Finding Meaning in the Fog

DEAR CREATIVE,

During our wilderness period, we often encounter "the fog." It's that disorienting place where you can't see ahead or behind, and you're unsure of what's going on or where to go next. In moments like this, instead of recklessly pushing forward and risking a crash—or forcing yourself further off course—it's often best to wait it out. Let the fog clear. You don't have to be on "go" all the time. We aren't performative machines that must create every single second. It's okay to pause, breathe, and take a moment.

Your wilderness period is an opportunity to stop and evaluate your surroundings. When the fog fades, you'll see a clear path forward. Don't view this as a punishment—it's more like a signal that some changes need to happen. It's time to check in with yourself. Ask: What is this wilderness period trying to tell me? How can I find meaning in the fog?

If you're feeling foggy, don't leap. Sit down and reflect. The path will clear for you soon.

— CRYSTAL

DEAR CREATIVE,

CHAPTER AFFIRMATIONS

Clarity will come, even when the path ahead feels unclear.

I trust that this foggy season is shaping me in meaningful ways.

I am open to discovering purpose, even in unexpected places.

DEAR CREATIVE,

Writing Prompts

DEAR CREATIVE,

DATE:

UNEXPECTED POSITIVES

What unexpected positives have come out of this wilderness period? Write about any silver linings you've found.

NEW INSIGHTS

How has this time changed your perspective on your creative journey? What new insights have you gained?

REFLECTION

What is one lesson you've learned during this wilderness period that you can carry forward? Describe how you plan to apply it in the future.

PROMPT

DATE:

Take some time to reflect on the songs that resonate with you during this season. Choose 4-6 lines from different songs that speak to your feelings, hopes, or struggles right now.

Write the lines down and arrange them to form your own verse. Let them flow together in a way that feels meaningful to you.

If you feel inspired, add a line or two of your own to tie the lyrics together.

After you've created your verse, write a few sentences about why you chose these lyrics and what they mean to you in this moment.

This is your opportunity to create something beautiful and personal from the words that already bring you comfort.

CREATIVE PROGRESS TRACKER

DATE:

This tracker is meant to help you track the small steps you take, even if creativity feels absent. It's not about the outcome, but the willingness to show up for yourself each day. If you can't create today, that's okay. Just take note of how you're feeling and what's showing up for you.

Instructions:

- *Instead of focusing on finished projects, use this space to reflect on your emotional state and any subtle moments of creative inspiration, even if they're fleeting.*

- *You don't have to create something every day. This is about honoring your process, not rushing or pushing yourself.*

What I Felt This Week	Creative Moments (Even Small Ones)	Challenges/ Barriers	What I've Learned About Myself	Gentle Next Step

Reflection Prompts:

How do I feel today about my creative process?

What is one small thing I can do for myself today, without expectation of producing anything?

What would it feel like to release the pressure of needing to create right now?

MOOD TRACKER

DATE:

This tracker helps you reflect on how you're feeling each day. Remember, it's okay if some days feel off or if inspiration isn't flowing. Your mood is part of your process and it's important to honor it.

Instructions:

Choose a color for each mood.
For each day, color in the corresponding mood based on how you felt.
At the end of the week, reflect on your emotional landscape. Notice patterns, but don't pressure yourself to always be "productive." Sometimes rest is the most important part of the journey.

Mood Key	Mood	Notes
● Inspired ● Calm ● Low ● Uncertain ● Sad		

Mood Key Colors:

● *Inspired -*
● *Calm -*
● *Low -*
● *Uncertain -*
● *Sad -*

DEAR CREATIVE,

You Are Enough

DEAR CREATIVE,

You are enough—right now. Not once you get that degree, not once you land that opportunity or scholarship, and not once you secure funding for your project. You alone are enough. The sooner you truly embrace this, the easier your wilderness period will feel. Yes, we love money, funding, and education. They're beautiful tools that can enhance our gifts and help us reach new levels. But even if you never receive another dime for your art, you are worthy. Your art is worthy.

Stop waiting for some magical solution—just start. Someone is waiting for your art. Someone needs to read your book, see your film, or hear your music. What you create is important right now. So even if you never gain another resource or accolade, don't stop creating. You are enough.

— CRYSTAL

DEAR CREATIVE,

CHAPTER AFFIRMATIONS

I am enough, just as I am, in this very moment.

My worth is not dependent on my achievements or circumstances.

I embrace my journey, knowing I am whole and complete.

DEAR CREATIVE,

Writing Prompts

DEAR CREATIVE,

DATE:

TALK YO ISH!

Write about a project or piece of work you are proud of. What skills and talents did you use to create it?

ROOM FOR IMPROVEMENT

List three areas where you want to improve and create a plan for how you can work on them.

REFLECTION

Reflect on a time when you doubted your talent but still pushed through. What was the outcome, and what did you learn?

PROMPT

DATE:

Create a visual reminder of your worth using affirmations, quotes, and images.

Write down or cut out affirmations that resonate with the idea that you are enough just as you are. These can come from this journal, your own thoughts, or external sources like books, songs, or quotes.

Gather old magazines, printed images, or draw symbols that represent self-love, strength, and acceptance.

On a blank page in your journal, arrange the affirmations and images in a way that feels empowering to you. Glue, tape, or draw them onto the page.

Add a personal touch: write your name boldly in the center or a phrase like "I Am Enough" to anchor the collage. Let this page serve as a reminder to turn to whenever you feel uncertain or need encouragement.

Take a moment to reflect on how you felt while creating your affirmation collage.

What emotions came up as you chose your affirmations and images?

Did any particular words or visuals resonate with you deeply?

How did this activity make you feel about yourself and your journey?

Do you feel more connected to the idea that you are enough?

Write your thoughts and feelings below. There's no right or wrong way—just be honest with yourself. This reflection is for you.

_____
_____
_____
_____
_____
_____
_____
_____

CREATIVE PROGRESS TRACKER

DATE:

This tracker is meant to help you track the small steps you take, even if creativity feels absent. It's not about the outcome, but the willingness to show up for yourself each day. If you can't create today, that's okay. Just take note of how you're feeling and what's showing up for you.

Instructions:

- *Instead of focusing on finished projects, use this space to reflect on your emotional state and any subtle moments of creative inspiration, even if they're fleeting.*

- *You don't have to create something every day. This is about honoring your process, not rushing or pushing yourself.*

What I Felt This Week	Creative Moments (Even Small Ones)	Challenges/ Barriers	What I've Learned About Myself	Gentle Next Step

Reflection Prompts:

How do I feel today about my creative process?

What is one small thing I can do for myself today, without expectation of producing anything?

What would it feel like to release the pressure of needing to create right now?

MOOD TRACKER

DATE :

This tracker helps you reflect on how you're feeling each day. Remember, it's okay if some days feel off or if inspiration isn't flowing. Your mood is part of your process and it's important to honor it.

Instructions:

Choose a color for each mood.
For each day, color in the corresponding mood based on how you felt.
At the end of the week, reflect on your emotional landscape. Notice patterns, but don't pressure yourself to always be "productive." Sometimes rest is the most important part of the journey.

Mood Key	Mood	Notes
● Inspired ● Calm ● Low ● Uncertain ● Sad		

Mood Key Colors:

● *Inspired -*
● *Calm -*
● *Low -*
● *Uncertain -*
● *Sad -*

DEAR CREATIVE,

Embracing Growth and Transformation

DEAR CREATIVE,

Growth and transformation are essential parts of the human experience, especially for creatives. But let's be real—it often feels like a challenge nobody asked for. Transformation pushes us closer to our highest selves, yet it demands the one thing most people resist: change.

Even though change is inevitable, it's something I've always struggled to embrace. I love feeling steady and secure. I love a good routine. I love being in control of what's happening around me. But change? It disrupts all those beautiful comforts. During your wilderness period, you'll likely feel completely out of control and at times your life will be unrecognizable.

Let it happen. Discomfort is part of the process, and your breakthrough is waiting on the other side.

— CRYSTAL

DEAR CREATIVE,

CHAPTER AFFIRMATIONS

I welcome change as a natural part of my evolution.

Growth may feel uncomfortable, but it is leading me to something greater.

I am transforming into the person I am meant to be.

DEAR CREATIVE,

Writing Prompts

DEAR CREATIVE,

DATE:

CREATIVE GOALS	REINTEGRATING CREATIVITY
How have your creative goals or aspirations shifted during this time? Write about any changes or new directions.	*What aspects of your creative practice have you been neglecting? How can you reintegrate them into your routine?*

REFLECTION

How can you transform this time into an opportunity for growth? List three actionable steps you can take.

PROMPT

DATE:

Draw or write about yourself as if you were a tree experiencing the four seasons. What does your spring of growth look like? How does summer feel when you're thriving? What falls away in autumn, and what does winter teach you about stillness and resilience?

CREATIVE PROGRESS TRACKER

DATE:

This tracker is meant to help you track the small steps you take, even if creativity feels absent. It's not about the outcome, but the willingness to show up for yourself each day. If you can't create today, that's okay. Just take note of how you're feeling and what's showing up for you.

Instructions:

- Instead of focusing on finished projects, use this space to reflect on your emotional state and any subtle moments of creative inspiration, even if they're fleeting.

- You don't have to create something every day. This is about honoring your process, not rushing or pushing yourself.

What I Felt This Week	Creative Moments (Even Small Ones)	Challenges/ Barriers	What I've Learned About Myself	Gentle Next Step

Reflection Prompts:

How do I feel today about my creative process?

What is one small thing I can do for myself today, without expectation of producing anything?

What would it feel like to release the pressure of needing to create right now?

MOOD TRACKER

DATE :

This tracker helps you reflect on how you're feeling each day. Remember, it's okay if some days feel off or if inspiration isn't flowing. Your mood is part of your process and it's important to honor it.

Instructions:

Choose a color for each mood.
For each day, color in the corresponding mood based on how you felt.
At the end of the week, reflect on your emotional landscape. Notice patterns, but don't pressure yourself to always be "productive." Sometimes rest is the most important part of the journey.

Mood Key	Mood	Notes
● Inspired ● Calm ● Low ● Uncertain ● Sad		

Mood Key Colors:

● *Inspired -*
● *Calm -*
● *Low -*
● *Uncertain -*
● *Sad -*

DEAR CREATIVE,

Moments of Reflection and Self Discovery

DEAR CREATIVE,

It's not always easy to look back on how things used to be—or even the person you once were—but exploring the past from an introspective place can completely shift how you move forward. After going through a wilderness period, you'll often realize you don't even feel like the same person anymore. And you're not. The growth and transformation you've experienced are life-changing, requiring you to get to know yourself all over again—especially as a creative.

The way you connect with your art and creativity may change drastically during this time. It can be heartbreaking to let go of the version of you that once existed, allowing that part of you to essentially die. But this is also an opportunity. Take time to reflect on everything you've been through and how it's reshaped you. How can you fully show up as this new version of yourself? How can you honor the creative evolution you've experienced? Let this be a moment of renewal.

— CRYSTAL

DEAR CREATIVE,

CHAPTER AFFIRMATIONS

Reflection helps me understand myself more deeply.

I am learning to love and accept all parts of who I am.

Every moment of self-discovery brings me closer to my true self.

DEAR CREATIVE,

Writing Prompts

DEAR CREATIVE,

DATE:

SELF-DISCOVERY	CREATIVE OUTPUT
Write about a moment of self-discovery you've had during this wilderness period. What did you learn about yourself?	*How has this period of introspection influenced your creative work? Reflect on any changes in your creative output.*

REFLECTION

What new habits or practices have you adopted during this time that have helped you? How can you maintain them moving forward?

PROMPT

DATE:

Look into a mirror and draw what you see. Write about any discomfort or revelations that arise from this exercise.

CREATIVE PROGRESS TRACKER

DATE:

This tracker is meant to help you track the small steps you take, even if creativity feels absent. It's not about the outcome, but the willingness to show up for yourself each day. If you can't create today, that's okay. Just take note of how you're feeling and what's showing up for you.

Instructions:

- *Instead of focusing on finished projects, use this space to reflect on your emotional state and any subtle moments of creative inspiration, even if they're fleeting.*

- *You don't have to create something every day. This is about honoring your process, not rushing or pushing yourself.*

What I Felt This Week	Creative Moments (Even Small Ones)	Challenges/ Barriers	What I've Learned About Myself	Gentle Next Step

Reflection Prompts:

How do I feel today about my creative process?

What is one small thing I can do for myself today, without expectation of producing anything?

What would it feel like to release the pressure of needing to create right now?

MOOD TRACKER

DATE:

This tracker helps you reflect on how you're feeling each day. Remember, it's okay if some days feel off or if inspiration isn't flowing. Your mood is part of your process and it's important to honor it.

Instructions:

Choose a color for each mood.
For each day, color in the corresponding mood based on how you felt.
At the end of the week, reflect on your emotional landscape. Notice patterns, but don't pressure yourself to always be "productive." Sometimes rest is the most important part of the journey.

Mood Key	Mood	Notes
● Inspired ● Calm ● Low ● Uncertain ● Sad		

Mood Key Colors:

● *Inspired -*
● *Calm -*
● *Low -*
● *Uncertain -*
● *Sad -*

DEAR CREATIVE,

Finding Clarity in Uncertainty

DEAR CREATIVE,

Plot Twist: You don't have to have it all figured out. We drive ourselves crazy trying to plan every little detail of our lives when, truthfully, some things are meant to unfold naturally through the human experience. For those of us who struggle with letting go of control, this can be one of the hardest parts of the wilderness period. Not knowing what happens next feels excruciating. There are no clues, no hints—just you, drowning in a sea of uncertainty. And it doesn't feel good.

But fret not—there is clarity in the chaos. This time of uncertainty gives you the opportunity to yield to divine timing and surrender. Things are unfolding exactly as they're meant to, and no, you don't know what's coming next... but **Spoiler Alert:** You win.

— CRYSTAL

DEAR CREATIVE,

CHAPTER AFFIRMATIONS

Even in uncertainty, I am finding my way.

I trust that clarity will reveal itself in due time.

The unknown is not my enemy; it is my guide.

DEAR CREATIVE,

Writing Prompts

DEAR CREATIVE,

DATE:

PERSPECTIVE SHIFTS

In what ways has this wilderness period clarified your values and priorities? Write about any shifts in your perspective.

BECOMING RESOURCEFUL

How has facing uncertainty helped you become more adaptable or resourceful? Reflect on specific instances.

REFLECTION

What small victories have you achieved despite the wilderness period? Write about these moments and what they taught you.

PROMPT

DATE:

Let's take a moment to explore something you're still uncertain about on your creative journey. What is it that's weighing on your mind or making you feel unsure? Be honest with yourself and walk through those feelings. What about it feels daunting or unclear? Are there fears or doubts holding you back? And most importantly, how can you begin to shift your perspective to embrace this uncertainty as part of the process? Remember, clarity often comes from sitting with the unknown and giving yourself the grace to figure it out in your own time.

CREATIVE PROGRESS TRACKER

DATE:

This tracker is meant to help you track the small steps you take, even if creativity feels absent. It's not about the outcome, but the willingness to show up for yourself each day. If you can't create today, that's okay. Just take note of how you're feeling and what's showing up for you.

Instructions:

- Instead of focusing on finished projects, use this space to reflect on your emotional state and any subtle moments of creative inspiration, even if they're fleeting.

- You don't have to create something every day. This is about honoring your process, not rushing or pushing yourself.

What I Felt This Week	Creative Moments (Even Small Ones)	Challenges/ Barriers	What I've Learned About Myself	Gentle Next Step

Reflection Prompts:

How do I feel today about my creative process?

What is one small thing I can do for myself today, without expectation of producing anything?

What would it feel like to release the pressure of needing to create right now?

MOOD TRACKER

DATE :

This tracker helps you reflect on how you're feeling each day. Remember, it's okay if some days feel off or if inspiration isn't flowing. Your mood is part of your process and it's important to honor it.

Instructions:

Choose a color for each mood.
For each day, color in the corresponding mood based on how you felt.
At the end of the week, reflect on your emotional landscape. Notice patterns, but don't pressure yourself to always be "productive." Sometimes rest is the most important part of the journey.

Mood Key	Mood	Notes
● Inspired ● Calm ● Low ● Uncertain ● Sad		

Mood Key Colors:

● *Inspired -*
● *Calm -*
● *Low -*
● *Uncertain -*
● *Sad -*

DEAR CREATIVE,

Gaining Insight from Challenges

DEAR CREATIVE,

When you're in the middle of a challenge, no one's sitting there thinking, "Hmm, I wonder what I'll learn from this." That's why they say hindsight is 20/20—it takes time to uncover the lessons our struggles are trying to teach us, and often, that clarity won't come until we're on the other side of them.

Wilderness periods can leave you utterly exhausted, tired of the endless challenges and the lessons that seem to tag along with them. But here's the thing: gaining insight from those challenges is part of what shapes you. It's how you grow, how you transform, and how you eventually find the strength to keep going.

— CRYSTAL

DEAR CREATIVE,

CHAPTER AFFIRMATIONS

Challenges are opportunities for me to learn and grow.

I am resilient and capable of overcoming anything life presents to me.

Each challenge holds a valuable lesson that strengthens me.

DEAR CREATIVE,

Writing Prompts

DEAR CREATIVE,

DATE:

MAIN CHALLENGES

What is the biggest challenge you've faced during this time, and what have you learned from it?

EMOTIONAL GROWTH

How have you grown emotionally and mentally during this period? Write about any personal development.

REFLECTION

Think of a time when you overcame a difficult situation. What lessons did that experience teach you about yourself, your resilience, or your creative process?

PROMPT

DATE:

Draw or write about a "scar" (physical, emotional, or metaphorical) that represents a past challenge. How has it contributed to your growth or taught you something valuable about yourself?

CREATIVE PROGRESS TRACKER

DATE:

This tracker is meant to help you track the small steps you take, even if creativity feels absent. It's not about the outcome, but the willingness to show up for yourself each day. If you can't create today, that's okay. Just take note of how you're feeling and what's showing up for you.

Instructions:

- Instead of focusing on finished projects, use this space to reflect on your emotional state and any subtle moments of creative inspiration, even if they're fleeting.

- You don't have to create something every day. This is about honoring your process, not rushing or pushing yourself.

What I Felt This Week	Creative Moments (Even Small Ones)	Challenges/ Barriers	What I've Learned About Myself	Gentle Next Step

Reflection Prompts:

How do I feel today about my creative process?

What is one small thing I can do for myself today, without expectation of producing anything?

What would it feel like to release the pressure of needing to create right now?

MOOD TRACKER

DATE :

This tracker helps you reflect on how you're feeling each day. Remember, it's okay if some days feel off or if inspiration isn't flowing. Your mood is part of your process and it's important to honor it.

Instructions:

Choose a color for each mood.
For each day, color in the corresponding mood based on how you felt.
At the end of the week, reflect on your emotional landscape. Notice patterns, but don't pressure yourself to always be "productive." Sometimes rest is the most important part of the journey.

Mood Key	Mood	Notes
● Inspired ● Calm ● Low ● Uncertain ● Sad		

Mood Key Colors:

● *Inspired -*
● *Calm -*
● *Low -*
● *Uncertain -*
● *Sad -*

DEAR CREATIVE,

Self-Compassion and Patience

DEAR CREATIVE,

Creating isn't easy. I know social media can make it seem effortless, but the truth is, it takes a lot of energy and effort—even when it comes naturally to you. During your wilderness period, you might encounter writer's block or, worse, what I call "creative burnout." Unlike a block, burnout doesn't stop your ideas from coming; it just steals the inspiration to bring them to life. Your mojo is gone, and you don't feel motivated to create anything. And here's the kicker: there's absolutely nothing you can do to speed it up.

But that's okay. Let yourself go through it. Don't force something out just because you feel like you have to. The beauty of creativity lies in the passion and heart we pour into it. Without that, it's just a soulless product—and nobody wants that.

If you're facing a block or burnout, be patient with yourself. There's nothing wrong with you. You haven't lost your secret sauce; you're simply going through a pivotal process that's setting the stage for something greater. Give yourself grace. This is a moment of transformation, and it's okay if you're not in the mood to create right now. Trust the process—it's about to change the trajectory of your life forever.

— CRYSTAL

DEAR CREATIVE,

CHAPTER AFFIRMATIONS

I trust in my own growth and honor the pace of my journey.

I show myself compassion, embracing both my strengths and my struggles.

I trust that all things are unfolding as they should, and I am patient with myself through the process.

DEAR CREATIVE,

Writing Prompts

DATE:

DEAR CREATIVE,

MAIN CHALLENGES

How can you practice self-compassion during this wilderness period? Write about ways to be kind to yourself.

EMOTIONAL GROWTH

What does patience look like for you in this period? Reflect on how you can cultivate more patience with yourself and your process.

REFLECTION

Think about a mistake you've made recently. How can you forgive yourself for it and view it as a learning opportunity? Write about the lessons gained from this mistake and how you can apply them moving forward.

PROMPT

DATE :

Draw or imagine a tree growing strong and steady. Label its roots with the values or practices that help you stay grounded, like self-compassion or mindfulness. Write on the branches the goals or dreams you're nurturing with patience.

CREATIVE PROGRESS TRACKER

DATE:

This tracker is meant to help you track the small steps you take, even if creativity feels absent. It's not about the outcome, but the willingness to show up for yourself each day. If you can't create today, that's okay. Just take note of how you're feeling and what's showing up for you.

Instructions:

- *Instead of focusing on finished projects, use this space to reflect on your emotional state and any subtle moments of creative inspiration, even if they're fleeting.*

- *You don't have to create something every day. This is about honoring your process, not rushing or pushing yourself.*

What I Felt This Week	Creative Moments (Even Small Ones)	Challenges/ Barriers	What I've Learned About Myself	Gentle Next Step

Reflection Prompts:

How do I feel today about my creative process?

What is one small thing I can do for myself today, without expectation of producing anything?

What would it feel like to release the pressure of needing to create right now?

MOOD TRACKER

DATE :

This tracker helps you reflect on how you're feeling each day. Remember, it's okay if some days feel off or if inspiration isn't flowing. Your mood is part of your process and it's important to honor it.

Instructions:

Choose a color for each mood.
For each day, color in the corresponding mood based on how you felt.
At the end of the week, reflect on your emotional landscape. Notice patterns, but don't pressure yourself to always be "productive." Sometimes rest is the most important part of the journey.

Mood Key	Mood	Notes
● Inspired ● Calm ● Low ● Uncertain ● Sad		

Mood Key Colors:

● *Inspired -*
● *Calm -*
● *Low -*
● *Uncertain -*
● *Sad -*

DEAR CREATIVE,

Mindfulness and Presence

DEAR CREATIVE,

There's no guidebook for navigating a wilderness period, but being present and practicing mindfulness is one of the best ways to center yourself and stay grounded—or as grounded as possible during a turbulent storm. It's tempting to detach when things feel uncomfortable, but that temporary numbness doesn't heal anything. It just delays the process and keeps you stuck. The purpose of your wilderness period is to help you tap into yourself, not avoid the hard stuff.

There are so many ways to center yourself during this time, and it's important to find what works for you. Personally, I love journaling and listening to music, but I know everyone's process looks different. Meditation, for example, isn't always about sitting in total silence for me—it's about quieting my mind in whatever way I can. You don't have to follow some ritualistic blueprint for calming your spirit.

Whether it's meditation, prayer, music, or even throwing that thang in a circle, do whatever reconnects you to yourself. The goal is to find your way back to the parts of you that feel steady, even in the chaos.

— CRYSTAL

DEAR CREATIVE,

CHAPTER AFFIRMATIONS

I choose to be present in this moment, as it is all I truly have.

Mindfulness helps me find peace, even in chaos.

I honor my journey by staying grounded and centered.

DEAR CREATIVE,

Writing Prompts

DEAR CREATIVE,

DATE:

INCORPORATING MINDFULNESS

How can you incorporate mindfulness into your daily routine to help navigate this period? List a few practices to try.

MOOD AND CREATIVITY

Write about a recent moment when you felt fully present. How did it affect your mood and creativity?

REFLECTION

Is there something you're avoiding or suppressing right now? How can mindfulness help you face it with more acceptance and less fear?

PROMPT

DATE:

Take a few minutes—no more than five—to do something that calms your spirit. It could be journaling, listening to your favorite song, meditating, or even dancing. Before you start, check in with yourself and note how you're feeling. As you engage in the activity, pay attention to what's happening in your mind and body. Then, when you're done, reflect on how you feel afterward.

What do you notice? Has anything shifted? Are you more grounded, more relaxed, or maybe even more energized? Use this time to connect with yourself and observe the power of small, intentional moments of calm.

CREATIVE PROGRESS TRACKER

DATE:

This tracker is meant to help you track the small steps you take, even if creativity feels absent. It's not about the outcome, but the willingness to show up for yourself each day. If you can't create today, that's okay. Just take note of how you're feeling and what's showing up for you.

Instructions:

- Instead of focusing on finished projects, use this space to reflect on your emotional state and any subtle moments of creative inspiration, even if they're fleeting.

- You don't have to create something every day. This is about honoring your process, not rushing or pushing yourself.

What I Felt This Week	Creative Moments (Even Small Ones)	Challenges/ Barriers	What I've Learned About Myself	Gentle Next Step

Reflection Prompts:

How do I feel today about my creative process?

What is one small thing I can do for myself today, without expectation of producing anything?

What would it feel like to release the pressure of needing to create right now?

MOOD TRACKER

DATE :

This tracker helps you reflect on how you're feeling each day. Remember, it's okay if some days feel off or if inspiration isn't flowing. Your mood is part of your process and it's important to honor it.

Instructions:

Choose a color for each mood.
For each day, color in the corresponding mood based on how you felt.
At the end of the week, reflect on your emotional landscape. Notice patterns, but don't pressure yourself to always be "productive." Sometimes rest is the most important part of the journey.

Mood Key	Mood	Notes
● Inspired ● Calm ● Low ● Uncertain ● Sad		

Mood Key Colors:

● *Inspired -*
● *Calm -*
● *Low -*
● *Uncertain -*
● *Sad -*

DEAR CREATIVE,

Reconnecting with Joy

DEAR CREATIVE,

Similarly to finding ways to center yourself, it's just as important to reconnect with a source of joy during this time. There will be days when you feel like giving up or quitting altogether, but identifying the things that genuinely make your soul glow can keep you going. Tap into your inner child energy—explore, play, and find what makes you smile. Just be mindful not to attach your joy to another person.

Yes, people can contribute to your happiness, but true joy is an inside job. When you stop assigning your happiness to someone else or expecting it to come from a relationship, you'll notice joy shows up more freely and frequently. That's because you're the one in control of it.

The life of a creative is full of ups and downs, but don't let the chaos keep you from reclaiming a little time for the things that make you happy. You deserve it. Joy is yours, and it's something no one else can take away.

Of course, there are moments when joy feels out of reach, and in those cases, consulting a licensed professional or physician is absolutely okay. Don't let anyone tell you to just pray or meditate your way through something when you need more support. Asking for help is a powerful act, and it's there for a reason—don't hesitate to use it.

— CRYSTAL

DEAR CREATIVE,

CHAPTER AFFIRMATIONS

Joy is always available to me, even in small moments.

I am worthy of happiness and deserve to experience it fully.

I find joy in rediscovering what lights up my soul.

DEAR CREATIVE,

Writing Prompts

DEAR CREATIVE,

DATE:

INCORPORATING MINDFULNESS

What activities bring you joy and relaxation? How can you incorporate more of them into your life?

MOOD AND CREATIVITY

Reflect on a time when you felt pure joy in your creative work. What were you doing, and how can you recreate that feeling?

REFLECTION

How can creativity help you reconnect with joy? Write about a creative project or activity that brings you a sense of joy, and explore ways to make space for more of it in your life.

PROMPT

DATE:

Create a collage of words, images, and/or colors that represent moments, activities, or memories that bring you joy. Use magazines, photos, or drawings to craft your visual celebration of happiness.

CREATIVE PROGRESS TRACKER

DATE :

This tracker is meant to help you track the small steps you take, even if creativity feels absent. It's not about the outcome, but the willingness to show up for yourself each day. If you can't create today, that's okay. Just take note of how you're feeling and what's showing up for you.

Instructions:

- Instead of focusing on finished projects, use this space to reflect on your emotional state and any subtle moments of creative inspiration, even if they're fleeting.

- You don't have to create something every day. This is about honoring your process, not rushing or pushing yourself.

What I Felt This Week	Creative Moments (Even Small Ones)	Challenges/ Barriers	What I've Learned About Myself	Gentle Next Step

Reflection Prompts:

How do I feel today about my creative process?

What is one small thing I can do for myself today, without expectation of producing anything?

What would it feel like to release the pressure of needing to create right now?

MOOD TRACKER

DATE :

This tracker helps you reflect on how you're feeling each day. Remember, it's okay if some days feel off or if inspiration isn't flowing. Your mood is part of your process and it's important to honor it.

Instructions:

Choose a color for each mood.
For each day, color in the corresponding mood based on how you felt.
At the end of the week, reflect on your emotional landscape. Notice patterns, but don't pressure yourself to always be "productive." Sometimes rest is the most important part of the journey.

Mood Key	Mood	Notes
● Inspired ● Calm ● Low ● Uncertain ● Sad		

Mood Key Colors:

● *Inspired -*
● *Calm -*
● *Low -*
● *Uncertain -*
● *Sad -*

DEAR CREATIVE,

Seeking Inspiration

DEAR CREATIVE,

I've mentioned before what I experienced during a creative burnout, and much of it centered around a lack of motivation or inspiration to create. While some people are able to use their wilderness period as creative fuel, it's not always easy to navigate one of the most deconstructive and turbulent times of your life and still feel inspired to make art. Often, the desire to create is completely absent when everything around you feels like it's spiraling.

Even if you don't feel like creating, it's crucial to find a source of inspiration to keep going. For me, that came from using my "downtime" to meet new people and build community. As an introvert with social anxiety, I typically create alone and stay to myself, but connecting with like-minded individuals who were also navigating similar challenges became an unexpected lifeline. It not only made the process easier, but also lit a fire in me. That connection reignited my drive and gave me the energy I needed to push past the lack of inspiration.

So, find something that inspires you. If creating isn't in the cards right now, maybe it's reading a new book, attending local events, or joining a community of people who share your passions. It doesn't have to be big, but stepping outside your creative bubble could spark the motivation you need to move forward.

— CRYSTAL

DEAR CREATIVE,

CHAPTER AFFIRMATIONS

Inspiration surrounds me, even in unexpected places.

I am open to new ideas and experiences that ignite my creativity.

My creativity flows freely when I trust my intuition and explore.

DEAR CREATIVE,

Writing Prompts

DEAR CREATIVE,

DATE:

INCORPORATING MINDFULNESS

Who or what inspires you during difficult times? Write about your sources of inspiration.

MOOD AND CREATIVITY

How can you seek out new experiences or perspectives to inspire your creativity? List a few ideas to explore.

REFLECTION

Think of a moment in your life where you felt awe or wonder—whether it was in nature, during a performance, or seeing something extraordinary. Write about how that feeling of awe can be a wellspring of inspiration for your creative journey.

PROMPT

DATE:

Create a visual map of things, places, and people that inspire you. This could be a literal map, a mood board, or a mind map of concepts. Don't overthink it—let your creativity guide you to things that spark a sense of wonder or excitement.

CREATIVE PROGRESS TRACKER

DATE:

This tracker is meant to help you track the small steps you take, even if creativity feels absent. It's not about the outcome, but the willingness to show up for yourself each day. If you can't create today, that's okay. Just take note of how you're feeling and what's showing up for you.

Instructions:

- *Instead of focusing on finished projects, use this space to reflect on your emotional state and any subtle moments of creative inspiration, even if they're fleeting.*

- *You don't have to create something every day. This is about honoring your process, not rushing or pushing yourself.*

What I Felt This Week	Creative Moments (Even Small Ones)	Challenges/ Barriers	What I've Learned About Myself	Gentle Next Step

Reflection Prompts:

How do I feel today about my creative process?

What is one small thing I can do for myself today, without expectation of producing anything?

What would it feel like to release the pressure of needing to create right now?

MOOD TRACKER

DATE :

This tracker helps you reflect on how you're feeling each day. Remember, it's okay if some days feel off or if inspiration isn't flowing. Your mood is part of your process and it's important to honor it.

Instructions:

Choose a color for each mood.
For each day, color in the corresponding mood based on how you felt.
At the end of the week, reflect on your emotional landscape. Notice patterns, but don't pressure yourself to always be "productive." Sometimes rest is the most important part of the journey.

Mood Key	Mood	Notes
● Inspired ● Calm ● Low ● Uncertain ● Sad		

Mood Key Colors:

● *Inspired -*
● *Calm -*
● *Low -*
● *Uncertain -*
● *Sad -*

DEAR CREATIVE,

Encouragement and Self-Care

DEAR CREATIVE,

There will absolutely be moments when you need encouragement, and it won't always come from someone else. That's why it's essential to find ways to pour into yourself. Self-care has become a bit of a buzzword synonymous with spa days, and while I'm all for a relaxing spa day with a mimosa and some good music, self-care is so much more than that.

It's about showing up for yourself in ways that nurture your mind, body, and spirit. Maybe it's journaling to process your thoughts, taking a much-needed vacation, or diving deep into shadow work to confront and heal the parts of yourself you often avoid. Whatever it is, be intentional about loving on yourself, because no one can do it better than you.

The world is hard enough. Make it a priority to care for yourself in ways that truly matter—ways that fill you up, make you feel whole, and remind you that you are your biggest advocate.

— CRYSTAL

DEAR CREATIVE,

CHAPTER AFFIRMATIONS

I pour into myself because I am deserving of care and love.

Encouragement starts within, and I choose to speak kindly to myself.

Taking care of myself is a priority, not a luxury.

DEAR CREATIVE,

Writing Prompts

DATE:

DEAR CREATIVE,

CELEBRATE SMALL WINS

Write down three small accomplishments or creative efforts you've made recently, even if they seem insignificant. How can you honor these wins?

POSITIVE AFFIRMATIONS

What are three positive statements you can tell yourself right now? Write them as if your biggest supporter is speaking directly to you.

REFLECTION

Why did you start this creative journey? Reflect on what ignited your passion in the beginning.

DEAR CREATIVE,

DATE:

RECONNECING WITH SELF

Describe your perfect self-care day. What activities help you recharge and reconnect with yourself?

WEEKLY SELF-CARE ROUTINE

List three self-care practices you can incorporate into your weekly routine to support your creativity. No matter how small.

REFLECTION

Do you ever feel guilty for taking time for yourself? Reflect on why you might feel guilty and write about how you can release that guilt in favor of nurturing your needs.

CREATIVE PROGRESS TRACKER

DATE:

This tracker is meant to help you track the small steps you take, even if creativity feels absent. It's not about the outcome, but the willingness to show up for yourself each day. If you can't create today, that's okay. Just take note of how you're feeling and what's showing up for you.

Instructions:

- Instead of focusing on finished projects, use this space to reflect on your emotional state and any subtle moments of creative inspiration, even if they're fleeting.

- You don't have to create something every day. This is about honoring your process, not rushing or pushing yourself.

What I Felt This Week	Creative Moments (Even Small Ones)	Challenges/ Barriers	What I've Learned About Myself	Gentle Next Step

Reflection Prompts:

How do I feel today about my creative process?

What is one small thing I can do for myself today, without expectation of producing anything?

What would it feel like to release the pressure of needing to create right now?

MOOD TRACKER

DATE :

This tracker helps you reflect on how you're feeling each day. Remember, it's okay if some days feel off or if inspiration isn't flowing. Your mood is part of your process and it's important to honor it.

Instructions:

Choose a color for each mood.
For each day, color in the corresponding mood based on how you felt.
At the end of the week, reflect on your emotional landscape. Notice patterns, but don't pressure yourself to always be "productive." Sometimes rest is the most important part of the journey.

Mood Key	Mood	Notes
● Inspired ● Calm ● Low ● Uncertain ● Sad		

Mood Key Colors:

● *Inspired -*
● *Calm -*
● *Low -*
● *Uncertain -*
● *Sad -*

DEAR CREATIVE,

Cultivating a Support System

DEAR CREATIVE,

Having a healthy support system is incredibly important, especially during your wilderness period. As someone who spends a lot of time alone, I can attest to how vital it is to have people you can turn to. It doesn't have to be a massive circle—even one or two people you can genuinely trust is invaluable.

During these moments of disconnection, when it feels like you're drifting from everything and everyone, knowing there are people who value, support, and love you can be a lifeline. And it doesn't have to be limited to close family or friends. There are so many ways to find community: joining a Facebook group or an online community of creatives, a fitness group, book club, church, sports team, or any shared interest.

The key is building connections that matter—people who pour into you as much as you pour into them. These equal energy exchanges are powerful and can make all the difference when navigating your toughest seasons.

— CRYSTAL

DEAR CREATIVE,

CHAPTER AFFIRMATIONS

I attract relationships that are nurturing and reciprocal.

I am not alone; I am supported and valued by those who care for me.

Building connections with others strengthens and uplifts me.

DEAR CREATIVE,

Writing Prompts

DEAR CREATIVE,

DATE:

REFLECTING ON PAST ACHIEVMENTS

CREATIVE TIMELINE

Who in your life supports your creative endeavors? Write about how they have impacted you.

How can you seek out new supportive connections in your creative community? List three actions you can take.

REFLECTION

How can you support others in your creative community? Reflect on how offering help can strengthen relationships and open doors to new connections.

PROMPT

DATE:

Consider the people who support you in ways that may not be immediately obvious. For example, a neighbor who checks in on you, a colleague who offers words of encouragement, or even the quiet energy of a loved one who trusts in your journey. Write about these unseen networks and how they contribute to your well-being.

CREATIVE PROGRESS TRACKER

DATE:

This tracker is meant to help you track the small steps you take, even if creativity feels absent. It's not about the outcome, but the willingness to show up for yourself each day. If you can't create today, that's okay. Just take note of how you're feeling and what's showing up for you.

Instructions:

- *Instead of focusing on finished projects, use this space to reflect on your emotional state and any subtle moments of creative inspiration, even if they're fleeting.*

- *You don't have to create something every day. This is about honoring your process, not rushing or pushing yourself.*

What I Felt This Week	Creative Moments (Even Small Ones)	Challenges/ Barriers	What I've Learned About Myself	Gentle Next Step

Reflection Prompts:

How do I feel today about my creative process?

What is one small thing I can do for myself today, without expectation of producing anything?

What would it feel like to release the pressure of needing to create right now?

MOOD TRACKER

DATE :

This tracker helps you reflect on how you're feeling each day. Remember, it's okay if some days feel off or if inspiration isn't flowing. Your mood is part of your process and it's important to honor it.

Instructions:

Choose a color for each mood.
For each day, color in the corresponding mood based on how you felt.
At the end of the week, reflect on your emotional landscape. Notice patterns, but don't pressure yourself to always be "productive." Sometimes rest is the most important part of the journey.

Mood Key	Mood	Notes
● Inspired ● Calm ● Low ● Uncertain ● Sad		

Mood Key Colors:

● Inspired -
● Calm -
● Low -
● Uncertain -
● Sad -

DEAR CREATIVE,

Embracing the Journey

DEAR CREATIVE,

There is no part of this wilderness period that is easy or predictable. It feels like a massive tornado tearing through your life, leaving you spinning and unsure of which way is up. As cliché as it may sound, the only thing you can do is buckle up and try to embrace the ride, because baby, it's happening, whether you're ready or not!

Embracing the journey might feel naive, but it's vital. The wilderness period is often just a fancy term for the dark night of the soul, but I want to be clear: this is not a punishment. It's a transformation, a reset, a powerful reckoning with yourself.

I don't want to glamorize it or make it seem like this is some dreamy, Instagram-worthy journey. It's not. It's messy, it's tough, and it challenges you to your core. But here's the thing: the wilderness period brings you closer—to your purpose, to your art, and most importantly, to yourself. Through all the chaos and pain, there's an incredible opportunity for rediscovery and growth. You're not just surviving this; you're becoming something stronger, more aligned, and ready to step into the next phase of your life.

— CRYSTAL

DEAR CREATIVE,

CHAPTER AFFIRMATIONS

I trust the process of my journey, even when it feels uncertain.

Every step I take, whether forward or backward, is a part of my growth.

My journey is uniquely mine, and I am proud of where it is taking me.

DEAR CREATIVE,

Writing Prompts

DEAR CREATIVE,

DATE:

FINDING YOUR WAY

Write about a time when you felt lost but eventually found your way. What helped you navigate through that period?

BECOMING

Reflect on the concept of "becoming." What does it mean to you, and how can you embrace this ongoing process in your creative life?

REFLECTION

How have you changed as a person since you first started pursuing your creative passions? Reflect on the growth you've experienced along the way.

PROMPT

DATE:

Let's explore the concept of "being present" on your journey. What does it mean to embrace the moment, even when the future feels uncertain? Write about the small victories or insights you've gained in the present and how they contribute to the bigger picture of your journey.

CREATIVE PROGRESS TRACKER

DATE:

This tracker is meant to help you track the small steps you take, even if creativity feels absent. It's not about the outcome, but the willingness to show up for yourself each day. If you can't create today, that's okay. Just take note of how you're feeling and what's showing up for you.

Instructions:

- *Instead of focusing on finished projects, use this space to reflect on your emotional state and any subtle moments of creative inspiration, even if they're fleeting.*

- *You don't have to create something every day. This is about honoring your process, not rushing or pushing yourself.*

What I Felt This Week	Creative Moments (Even Small Ones)	Challenges/ Barriers	What I've Learned About Myself	Gentle Next Step

Reflection Prompts:

How do I feel today about my creative process?

What is one small thing I can do for myself today, without expectation of producing anything?

What would it feel like to release the pressure of needing to create right now?

MOOD TRACKER

DATE:

This tracker helps you reflect on how you're feeling each day. Remember, it's okay if some days feel off or if inspiration isn't flowing. Your mood is part of your process and it's important to honor it.

Instructions:

Choose a color for each mood.
For each day, color in the corresponding mood based on how you felt.
At the end of the week, reflect on your emotional landscape. Notice patterns, but don't pressure yourself to always be "productive." Sometimes rest is the most important part of the journey.

Mood Key	Mood	Notes
● Inspired ● Calm ● Low ● Uncertain ● Sad		

Mood Key Colors:

● *Inspired -*
● *Calm -*
● *Low -*
● *Uncertain -*
● *Sad -*

DEAR CREATIVE,

Let's Get Creative

DEAR CREATIVE,

You've reached the end of this journal, but we both know that this is never really the end. The journey doesn't stop here. I hope my words and the prompts along the way have sparked something in you, and remember, you can always come back to these pages whenever you need a reminder of how far you've come.

This journal marks just one chapter of your story. The real magic happens in the unfolding of your journey, and I'm cheering you on as you continue to grow, heal, and create. Embrace each twist and turn, each challenge and breakthrough, for they're all part of your evolution.

On the following pages, I've included a few activities you can cut out and use, along with some blank spaces to let your thoughts flow freely. Whether you want to draw, journal, or simply reflect, make this space your own.

I'm sending you all the love and encouragement you need as you step into the next phase of your journey. Trust that your path is unfolding exactly as it's meant to, and I'll see you on the other side. Keep creating, keep evolving, and keep believing in the beauty of what's to come.

— CRYSTAL

DEAR CREATIVE,

CHAPTER AFFIRMATIONS

Creativity flows through me naturally and abundantly.

I give myself permission to create freely, without judgment or fear.

My art is an expression of my truth, and it is worthy of being shared.

DEAR CREATIVE,

Writing Prompts

PROMPT

DATE:

Listen to one the following songs: (yes, even if you've heard them a million times...humor me)

I'm Coming Back - Lalah Hathaway and Rachelle Ferrell
Sailing - Avant (cover)
Naima - John Coltrane
I Want to Thank You - Alicia Myers
The Answer is You - Phyllis Hyman
I Told the Storm - Greg O' Quin N' Joyful Noize
I Am Everything - Beautiful Chorus
Good Morning Gorgeous - Mary J. Blige
Spirit - Cleo Sol

Free write while you listen to the song. How does it make if you feel? What lyrics stand out? In this very moment, what does this song mean to you?

_____

_____

_____

_____

_____

_____

_____

_____

_____

_____

_____

_____

_____

PROMPT

DATE:

Imagine your life as a movie and create a soundtrack of (5) songs for your journey towards achieving your goals. Describe each song and its significance.

How does each song reflect a part of your journey?

PROMPT

DATE:

Create an album cover for your life's soundtrack. Draw or collage the cover and write about the theme of your album.

PROMPT

DATE:

Create a playlist of songs that inspire and motivate you. Write about how each song makes you feel.

PROMPT

DATE:

Spend 10 minutes drawing or doodling your current emotions. Reflect on what comes up for you during this exercise.

_____

_____

_____

_____

_____

PROMPT

DATE:

Write a dialogue between your conscious self and your shadow self. What does your shadow self want to tell you?

PROMPT

DATE:

Find a song that speaks to your hidden or suppressed emotions. Write about how the lyrics and melody resonate with your shadow self.

PROMPT

DATE:

Write a letter from your future self who has achieved your goals. What advice do they give you? How do they describe their life now?

PROMPT

DATE:

Set a timer for 10 minutes and write whatever comes to mind. Don't censor yourself or worry about grammar—just let the words flow. Afterward, read it back and underline anything that stands out or surprises you.

PROMPT

DATE:

Draw a large mirror on the page and write down the aspects of yourself you're working to understand or heal. Around the mirror, write affirmations of love and acceptance for those parts of you.

PROMPT

DATE:

Write or draw small things that bring you joy—books, movies, favorite snacks, hobbies, or places. Surround these images or words with doodles or colors that make you smile.

DEAR CREATIVE,

PROMPT

DATE:

Write about a moment you want to remember forever. What made it special? How did it make you feel? If you can, draw or attach something that represents that memory.

DEAR CREATIVE,

PROMPT

DATE:

Write down fears, doubts, or anything holding you back on a page. Rip it out, crumple it, and throw it away—or if safe, burn it. Release those feelings physically.

PROMPT

DATE:

Sketch a map of the people or communities in your life that pour into you. Label each connection with how they support or inspire you.

PROMPT

DATE:

Create a list or drawing of your "emotional survival kit" for the wilderness period. Include tools like affirmations, mindfulness practices, favorite songs, or quotes that uplift you.

DEAR CREATIVE,

PROMPT

DATE:

Below is a tree with growth rings. Assign each ring to a challenge, lesson, or transformation from your wilderness period. Reflect on how each layer has contributed to who you are now.

PROMPT

DATE :

Below are multiple paths diverging in the wilderness. Label each with a choice or opportunity that has presented itself to you. Reflect on which path you took (or will take) and why. Feel free to include more paths.

PROMPT

DATE:

Create a garden of grief on the page. Each plant represents something you've lost or had to let go of during this time. Reflect on what each plant means to you and how it has shaped your journey.

PROMPT

DATE :

Below is a bridge over a turbulent river in your wilderness. On one side, write what you're leaving behind. On the other, write what awaits you after crossing.

PROMPT

DATE:

Design a compass to guide you through your wilderness. Label the directions with values, emotions, or practices that keep you grounded (e.g., North = Truth, East = Peace).

PROMPT

DATE :

Imagine you're sending a postcard from the middle of your wilderness period. Draw the "view" and write a short note to your future self about what you're learning.

PROMPT

DATE:

Draw a mountain range where each peak represents a challenge or breakthrough you've experienced. Write about what it took to "climb" each one and how it changed you.

DEAR CREATIVE,

PROMPT

DATE:

Imagine you're standing in the wilderness and hear echoes of your past calling out to you. What are they saying? Write or draw what messages or lessons they're sending.

PROMPT

DATE:

Write about the "wildflowers" growing in your wilderness—unexpected joys, lessons, or moments of beauty. Illustrate them if you'd like!

PROMPT

DATE:

Design a sanctuary within your wilderness—a safe place where you can rest and recharge. Describe or draw what it looks like and how it makes you feel.

DEAR CREATIVE,

PROMPT

DATE :

What does this photo make you feel? Write a poem, phrase, or journal entry.

PROMPT

DATE:

What does this photo make you feel? Write a poem, phrase, or journal entry.

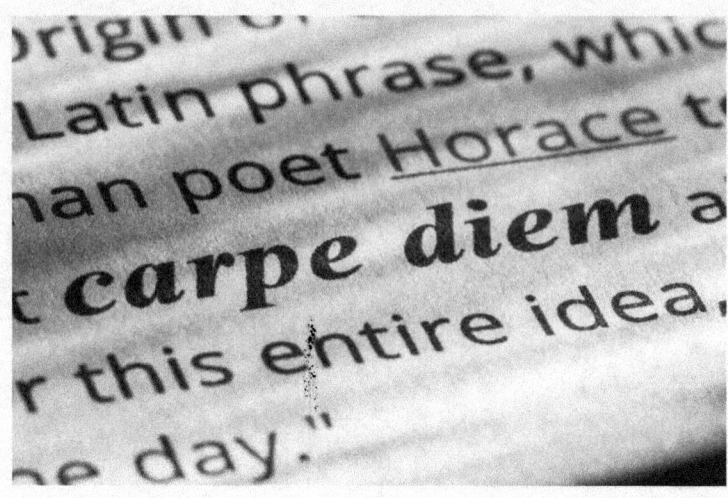

PROMPT

DATE:

What does this photo make you feel? Write a poem, phrase, or journal entry.

PROMPT

DATE:

What does this photo make you feel? Write a poem, phrase, or journal entry.

PROMPT

DATE :

What does this photo make you feel? Write a poem, phrase, or journal entry.

PROMPT

DATE:

What does this photo make you feel? Write a poem, phrase, or journal entry.

PROMPT

DATE:

What does this photo make you feel? Write a poem, phrase, or journal entry.

PROMPT

DATE:

What does this photo make you feel? Write a poem, phrase, or journal entry.

PROMPT

DATE:

What does this photo make you feel? Write a poem, phrase, or journal entry.

_____
_____
_____
_____
_____
_____
_____
_____
_____
_____
_____
_____

PROMPT

DATE:

What does this photo make you feel? Write a poem, phrase, or journal entry.

DEAR CREATIVE,

Creative Progress Trackers

CREATIVE PROGRESS TRACKER

DATE:

This tracker is meant to help you track the small steps you take, even if creativity feels absent. It's not about the outcome, but the willingness to show up for yourself each day. If you can't create today, that's okay. Just take note of how you're feeling and what's showing up for you.

Instructions:

- *Instead of focusing on finished projects, use this space to reflect on your emotional state and any subtle moments of creative inspiration, even if they're fleeting.*

- *You don't have to create something every day. This is about honoring your process, not rushing or pushing yourself.*

What I Felt This Week	Creative Moments (Even Small Ones)	Challenges/ Barriers	What I've Learned About Myself	Gentle Next Step

Reflection Prompts:

How do I feel today about my creative process?

What is one small thing I can do for myself today, without expectation of producing anything?

What would it feel like to release the pressure of needing to create right now?

CREATIVE PROGRESS TRACKER

DATE:

This tracker is meant to help you track the small steps you take, even if creativity feels absent. It's not about the outcome, but the willingness to show up for yourself each day. If you can't create today, that's okay. Just take note of how you're feeling and what's showing up for you.

Instructions:

- Instead of focusing on finished projects, use this space to reflect on your emotional state and any subtle moments of creative inspiration, even if they're fleeting.

- You don't have to create something every day. This is about honoring your process, not rushing or pushing yourself.

What I Felt This Week	Creative Moments (Even Small Ones)	Challenges/ Barriers	What I've Learned About Myself	Gentle Next Step

Reflection Prompts:

How do I feel today about my creative process?

What is one small thing I can do for myself today, without expectation of producing anything?

What would it feel like to release the pressure of needing to create right now?

CREATIVE PROGRESS TRACKER

DATE:

This tracker is meant to help you track the small steps you take, even if creativity feels absent. It's not about the outcome, but the willingness to show up for yourself each day. If you can't create today, that's okay. Just take note of how you're feeling and what's showing up for you.

Instructions:

- Instead of focusing on finished projects, use this space to reflect on your emotional state and any subtle moments of creative inspiration, even if they're fleeting.

- You don't have to create something every day. This is about honoring your process, not rushing or pushing yourself.

What I Felt This Week	Creative Moments (Even Small Ones)	Challenges/ Barriers	What I've Learned About Myself	Gentle Next Step

Reflection Prompts:

How do I feel today about my creative process?

What is one small thing I can do for myself today, without expectation of producing anything?

What would it feel like to release the pressure of needing to create right now?

CREATIVE PROGRESS TRACKER

DATE:

This tracker is meant to help you track the small steps you take, even if creativity feels absent. It's not about the outcome, but the willingness to show up for yourself each day. If you can't create today, that's okay. Just take note of how you're feeling and what's showing up for you.

Instructions:

- Instead of focusing on finished projects, use this space to reflect on your emotional state and any subtle moments of creative inspiration, even if they're fleeting.

- You don't have to create something every day. This is about honoring your process, not rushing or pushing yourself.

What I Felt This Week	Creative Moments (Even Small Ones)	Challenges/ Barriers	What I've Learned About Myself	Gentle Next Step

Reflection Prompts:

How do I feel today about my creative process?

What is one small thing I can do for myself today, without expectation of producing anything?

What would it feel like to release the pressure of needing to create right now?

CREATIVE PROGRESS TRACKER

DATE:

This tracker is meant to help you track the small steps you take, even if creativity feels absent. It's not about the outcome, but the willingness to show up for yourself each day. If you can't create today, that's okay. Just take note of how you're feeling and what's showing up for you.

Instructions:

- Instead of focusing on finished projects, use this space to reflect on your emotional state and any subtle moments of creative inspiration, even if they're fleeting.

- You don't have to create something every day. This is about honoring your process, not rushing or pushing yourself.

What I Felt This Week	Creative Moments (Even Small Ones)	Challenges/ Barriers	What I've Learned About Myself	Gentle Next Step

Reflection Prompts:

How do I feel today about my creative process?

What is one small thing I can do for myself today, without expectation of producing anything?

What would it feel like to release the pressure of needing to create right now?

CREATIVE PROGRESS TRACKER

DATE:

This tracker is meant to help you track the small steps you take, even if creativity feels absent. It's not about the outcome, but the willingness to show up for yourself each day. If you can't create today, that's okay. Just take note of how you're feeling and what's showing up for you.

Instructions:

- *Instead of focusing on finished projects, use this space to reflect on your emotional state and any subtle moments of creative inspiration, even if they're fleeting.*

- *You don't have to create something every day. This is about honoring your process, not rushing or pushing yourself.*

What I Felt This Week	Creative Moments (Even Small Ones)	Challenges/ Barriers	What I've Learned About Myself	Gentle Next Step

Reflection Prompts:

How do I feel today about my creative process?

What is one small thing I can do for myself today, without expectation of producing anything?

What would it feel like to release the pressure of needing to create right now?

CREATIVE PROGRESS TRACKER

DATE:

This tracker is meant to help you track the small steps you take, even if creativity feels absent. It's not about the outcome, but the willingness to show up for yourself each day. If you can't create today, that's okay. Just take note of how you're feeling and what's showing up for you.

Instructions:

- Instead of focusing on finished projects, use this space to reflect on your emotional state and any subtle moments of creative inspiration, even if they're fleeting.

- You don't have to create something every day. This is about honoring your process, not rushing or pushing yourself.

What I Felt This Week	Creative Moments (Even Small Ones)	Challenges/ Barriers	What I've Learned About Myself	Gentle Next Step

Reflection Prompts:

How do I feel today about my creative process?

What is one small thing I can do for myself today, without expectation of producing anything?

What would it feel like to release the pressure of needing to create right now?

CREATIVE PROGRESS TRACKER

DATE:

This tracker is meant to help you track the small steps you take, even if creativity feels absent. It's not about the outcome, but the willingness to show up for yourself each day. If you can't create today, that's okay. Just take note of how you're feeling and what's showing up for you.

Instructions:

- *Instead of focusing on finished projects, use this space to reflect on your emotional state and any subtle moments of creative inspiration, even if they're fleeting.*

- *You don't have to create something every day. This is about honoring your process, not rushing or pushing yourself.*

What I Felt This Week	Creative Moments (Even Small Ones)	Challenges/ Barriers	What I've Learned About Myself	Gentle Next Step

Reflection Prompts:

How do I feel today about my creative process?

What is one small thing I can do for myself today, without expectation of producing anything?

What would it feel like to release the pressure of needing to create right now?

CREATIVE PROGRESS TRACKER

DATE:

This tracker is meant to help you track the small steps you take, even if creativity feels absent. It's not about the outcome, but the willingness to show up for yourself each day. If you can't create today, that's okay. Just take note of how you're feeling and what's showing up for you.

Instructions:

- Instead of focusing on finished projects, use this space to reflect on your emotional state and any subtle moments of creative inspiration, even if they're fleeting.

- You don't have to create something every day. This is about honoring your process, not rushing or pushing yourself.

What I Felt This Week	Creative Moments (Even Small Ones)	Challenges/ Barriers	What I've Learned About Myself	Gentle Next Step

Reflection Prompts:

How do I feel today about my creative process?

What is one small thing I can do for myself today, without expectation of producing anything?

What would it feel like to release the pressure of needing to create right now?

CREATIVE PROGRESS TRACKER

DATE:

This tracker is meant to help you track the small steps you take, even if creativity feels absent. It's not about the outcome, but the willingness to show up for yourself each day. If you can't create today, that's okay. Just take note of how you're feeling and what's showing up for you.

Instructions:

- Instead of focusing on finished projects, use this space to reflect on your emotional state and any subtle moments of creative inspiration, even if they're fleeting.

- You don't have to create something every day. This is about honoring your process, not rushing or pushing yourself.

What I Felt This Week	Creative Moments (Even Small Ones)	Challenges/ Barriers	What I've Learned About Myself	Gentle Next Step

Reflection Prompts:

How do I feel today about my creative process?

What is one small thing I can do for myself today, without expectation of producing anything?

What would it feel like to release the pressure of needing to create right now?

DEAR CREATIVE,

Mood Trackers

MOOD TRACKER

DATE:

This tracker helps you reflect on how you're feeling each day. Remember, it's okay if some days feel off or if inspiration isn't flowing. Your mood is part of your process and it's important to honor it.

Instructions:

Choose a color for each mood.
For each day, color in the corresponding mood based on how you felt.
At the end of the week, reflect on your emotional landscape. Notice patterns, but don't pressure yourself to always be "productive." Sometimes rest is the most important part of the journey.

Mood Key	Mood	Notes
● Inspired ● Calm ● Low ● Uncertain ● Sad		

Mood Key Colors:

● Inspired -
● Calm -
● Low -
● Uncertain -
● Sad -

MOOD TRACKER

DATE:

This tracker helps you reflect on how you're feeling each day. Remember, it's okay if some days feel off or if inspiration isn't flowing. Your mood is part of your process and it's important to honor it.

Instructions:

Choose a color for each mood.
For each day, color in the corresponding mood based on how you felt.
At the end of the week, reflect on your emotional landscape. Notice patterns, but don't pressure yourself to always be "productive." Sometimes rest is the most important part of the journey.

Mood Key	Mood	Notes
● Inspired ● Calm ● Low ● Uncertain ● Sad		

Mood Key Colors:

● *Inspired -*
● *Calm -*
● *Low -*
● *Uncertain -*
● *Sad -*

MOOD TRACKER

DATE:

This tracker helps you reflect on how you're feeling each day. Remember, it's okay if some days feel off or if inspiration isn't flowing. Your mood is part of your process and it's important to honor it.

Instructions:

Choose a color for each mood.
For each day, color in the corresponding mood based on how you felt.
At the end of the week, reflect on your emotional landscape. Notice patterns, but don't pressure yourself to always be "productive." Sometimes rest is the most important part of the journey.

Mood Key	Mood	Notes
● Inspired ● Calm ● Low ● Uncertain ● Sad		

Mood Key Colors:

● Inspired -
● Calm -
● Low -
● Uncertain -
● Sad -

MOOD TRACKER

DATE:

This tracker helps you reflect on how you're feeling each day. Remember, it's okay if some days feel off or if inspiration isn't flowing. Your mood is part of your process and it's important to honor it.

Instructions:

Choose a color for each mood.
For each day, color in the corresponding mood based on how you felt.
At the end of the week, reflect on your emotional landscape. Notice patterns, but don't pressure yourself to always be "productive." Sometimes rest is the most important part of the journey.

Mood Key	Mood	Notes
● Inspired ● Calm ● Low ● Uncertain ● Sad		

Mood Key Colors:

● *Inspired -*
● *Calm -*
● *Low -*
● *Uncertain -*
● *Sad -*

MOOD TRACKER

DATE:

This tracker helps you reflect on how you're feeling each day. Remember, it's okay if some days feel off or if inspiration isn't flowing. Your mood is part of your process and it's important to honor it.

Instructions:

Choose a color for each mood.
For each day, color in the corresponding mood based on how you felt.
At the end of the week, reflect on your emotional landscape. Notice patterns, but don't pressure yourself to always be "productive." Sometimes rest is the most important part of the journey.

Mood Key	Mood	Notes
● Inspired ● Calm ● Low ● Uncertain ● Sad		

Mood Key Colors:

● Inspired -
● Calm -
● Low -
● Uncertain -
● Sad -

MOOD TRACKER

DATE:

This tracker helps you reflect on how you're feeling each day. Remember, it's okay if some days feel off or if inspiration isn't flowing. Your mood is part of your process and it's important to honor it.

Instructions:

Choose a color for each mood.
For each day, color in the corresponding mood based on how you felt.
At the end of the week, reflect on your emotional landscape. Notice patterns, but don't pressure yourself to always be "productive." Sometimes rest is the most important part of the journey.

Mood Key	Mood	Notes
● Inspired ● Calm ● Low ● Uncertain ● Sad		

Mood Key Colors:

● *Inspired -*
● *Calm -*
● *Low -*
● *Uncertain -*
● *Sad -*

MOOD TRACKER

DATE:

This tracker helps you reflect on how you're feeling each day. Remember, it's okay if some days feel off or if inspiration isn't flowing. Your mood is part of your process and it's important to honor it.

Instructions:

Choose a color for each mood.
For each day, color in the corresponding mood based on how you felt.
At the end of the week, reflect on your emotional landscape. Notice patterns, but don't pressure yourself to always be "productive." Sometimes rest is the most important part of the journey.

Mood Key	Mood	Notes
● Inspired ● Calm ● Low ● Uncertain ● Sad		

Mood Key Colors:

● Inspired -
● Calm -
● Low -
● Uncertain -
● Sad -

MOOD TRACKER

DATE :

This tracker helps you reflect on how you're feeling each day. Remember, it's okay if some days feel off or if inspiration isn't flowing. Your mood is part of your process and it's important to honor it.

Instructions:

Choose a color for each mood.
For each day, color in the corresponding mood based on how you felt.
At the end of the week, reflect on your emotional landscape. Notice patterns, but don't pressure yourself to always be "productive." Sometimes rest is the most important part of the journey.

Mood Key	Mood	Notes
● Inspired ● Calm ● Low ● Uncertain ● Sad		

Mood Key Colors:

● *Inspired -*
● *Calm -*
● *Low -*
● *Uncertain -*
● *Sad -*

MOOD TRACKER

DATE:

This tracker helps you reflect on how you're feeling each day. Remember, it's okay if some days feel off or if inspiration isn't flowing. Your mood is part of your process and it's important to honor it.

Instructions:

Choose a color for each mood.
For each day, color in the corresponding mood based on how you felt.
At the end of the week, reflect on your emotional landscape. Notice patterns, but don't pressure yourself to always be "productive." Sometimes rest is the most important part of the journey.

Mood Key	Mood	Notes
● Inspired ● Calm ● Low ● Uncertain ● Sad		

Mood Key Colors:

● *Inspired -*
● *Calm -*
● *Low -*
● *Uncertain -*
● *Sad -*

MOOD TRACKER

DATE :

This tracker helps you reflect on how you're feeling each day. Remember, it's okay if some days feel off or if inspiration isn't flowing. Your mood is part of your process and it's important to honor it.

Instructions:

Choose a color for each mood.
For each day, color in the corresponding mood based on how you felt.
At the end of the week, reflect on your emotional landscape. Notice patterns, but don't pressure yourself to always be "productive." Sometimes rest is the most important part of the journey.

Mood Key	Mood	Notes
● Inspired ● Calm ● Low ● Uncertain ● Sad		

Mood Key Colors:

● *Inspired -*
● *Calm -*
● *Low -*
● *Uncertain -*
● *Sad -*

DEAR CREATIVE,

Mood Markers

DEAR CREATIVE,

- fulfilled
- empowered
- resilient
- nurturing
- balanced
- inspired
- content
- grounded
- rejuvenated
- grateful
- aligned
- energized

DEAR CREATIVE,

DEAR CREATIVE,

confident	overwhelmed
connected	exhausted
purposeful	burnt-out
serene	frustrated
focused	anxious
optimistic	stagnant

DEAR CREATIVE,

DEAR CREATIVE,

- lost
- defeated
- disheartened
- helpless
- disconnected
- doubtful
- drained
- uncertain
- frantic
- lonely
- impatient
- worn-out

DEAR CREATIVE,

DEAR CREATIVE,

tense	mindful
unmotivated	luminous
at peace	hopeful
empathetic	gracious
vibrant	refreshed
self assured	transformed

DEAR CREATIVE,

DEAR CREATIVE,

centered	exasperated
curagious	supportive
sustained	overburdened
frustrated	isolated
vulnerable	unsettled
disappointed	insecure

DEAR CREATIVE,

DEAR CREATIVE,

unfulfilled	jaded
uneasy	numb
turbulent	desolate
empathetic	limitless
unseen	unstoppable
unstoppable	stagnant

DEAR CREATIVE,

DEAR CREATIVE,

- healthy
- whole
- badass
- unapologetic
- intentional
- cherished

- loveable
- deserving
- magical
- clear
- genius
- disciplined

DEAR CREATIVE,

DEAR CREATIVE,

abundant	blooming
succesful	capable
renewed	irresistible
undeniable	passionate
authentic	talented
indecisive	prosperous

DEAR CREATIVE,

DEAR CREATIVE,

Free Flow Pages

DEAR CREATIVE,

DEAR CREATIVE,

DEAR CREATIVE,

DEAR CREATIVE,

DEAR CREATIVE,

DEAR CREATIVE,

DEAR CREATIVE,

DEAR CREATIVE,

DEAR CREATIVE,

DEAR CREATIVE,

www.ingramcontent.com/pod-product-compliance
Lightning Source LLC
Chambersburg PA
CBHW081329230426
43667CB00018B/2872